AUSTRALIA'S REMARKABLE WILDLIFE

JOHN LESLEY

WOMBAT

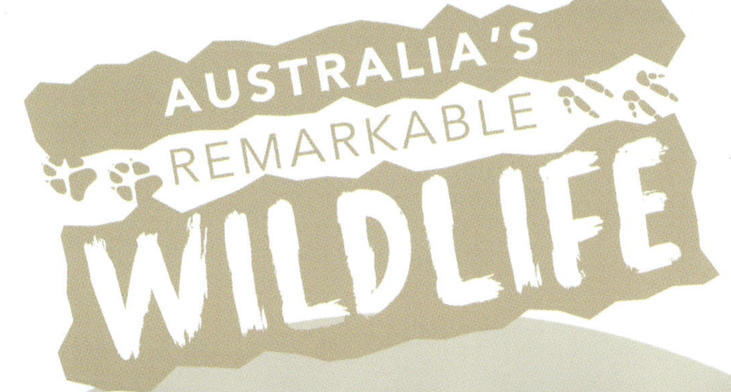

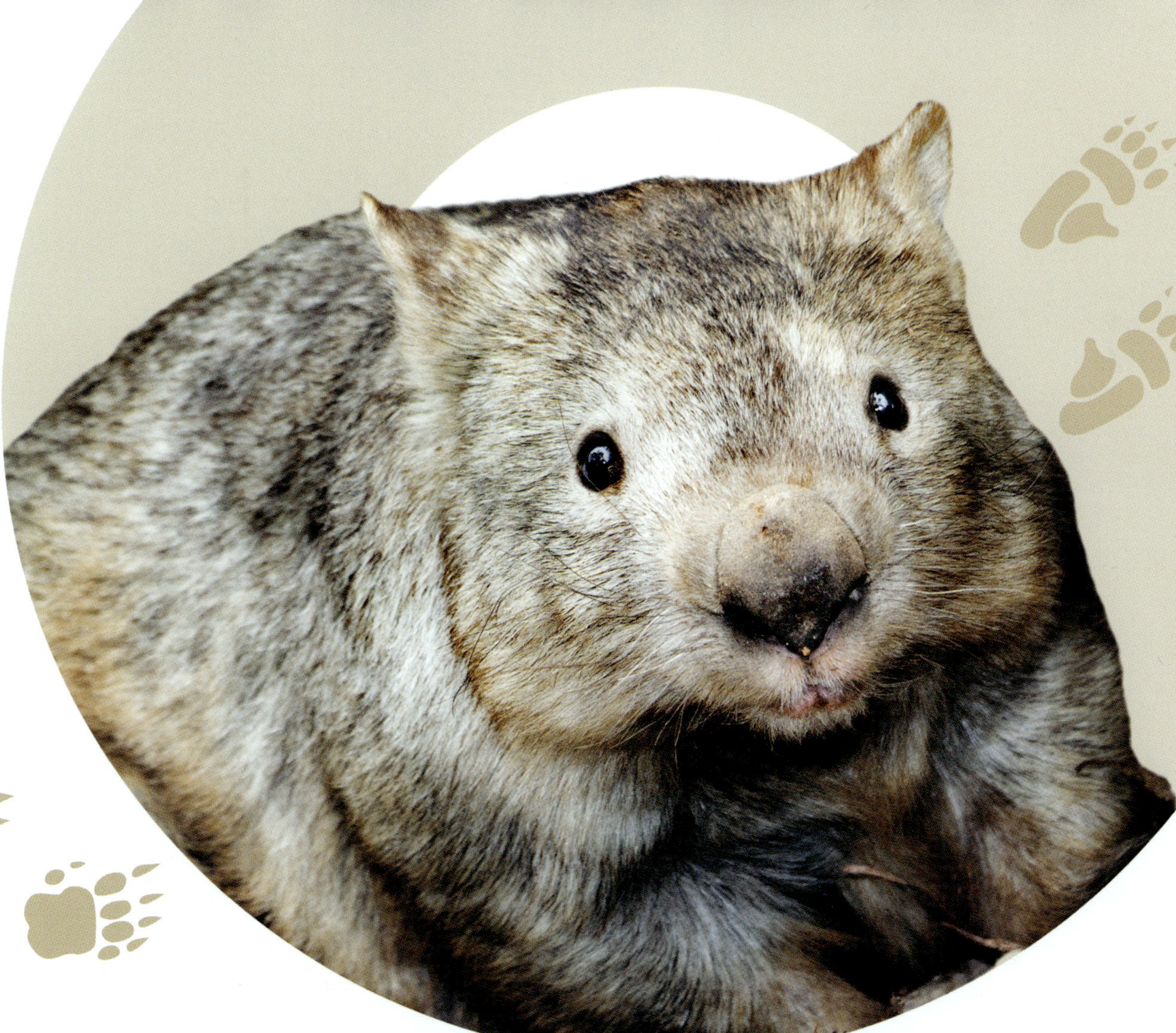

REDBACK publishing

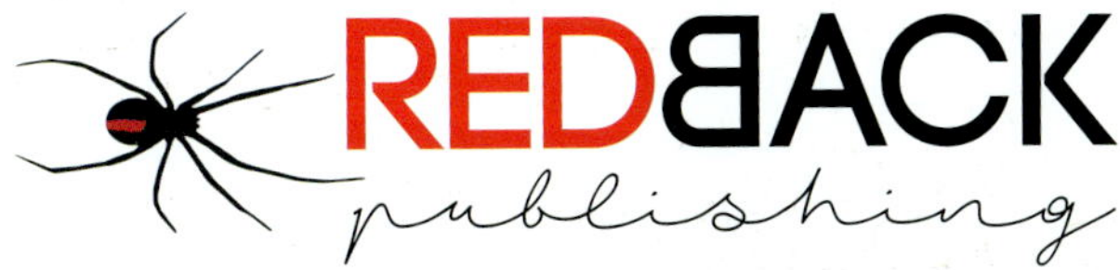

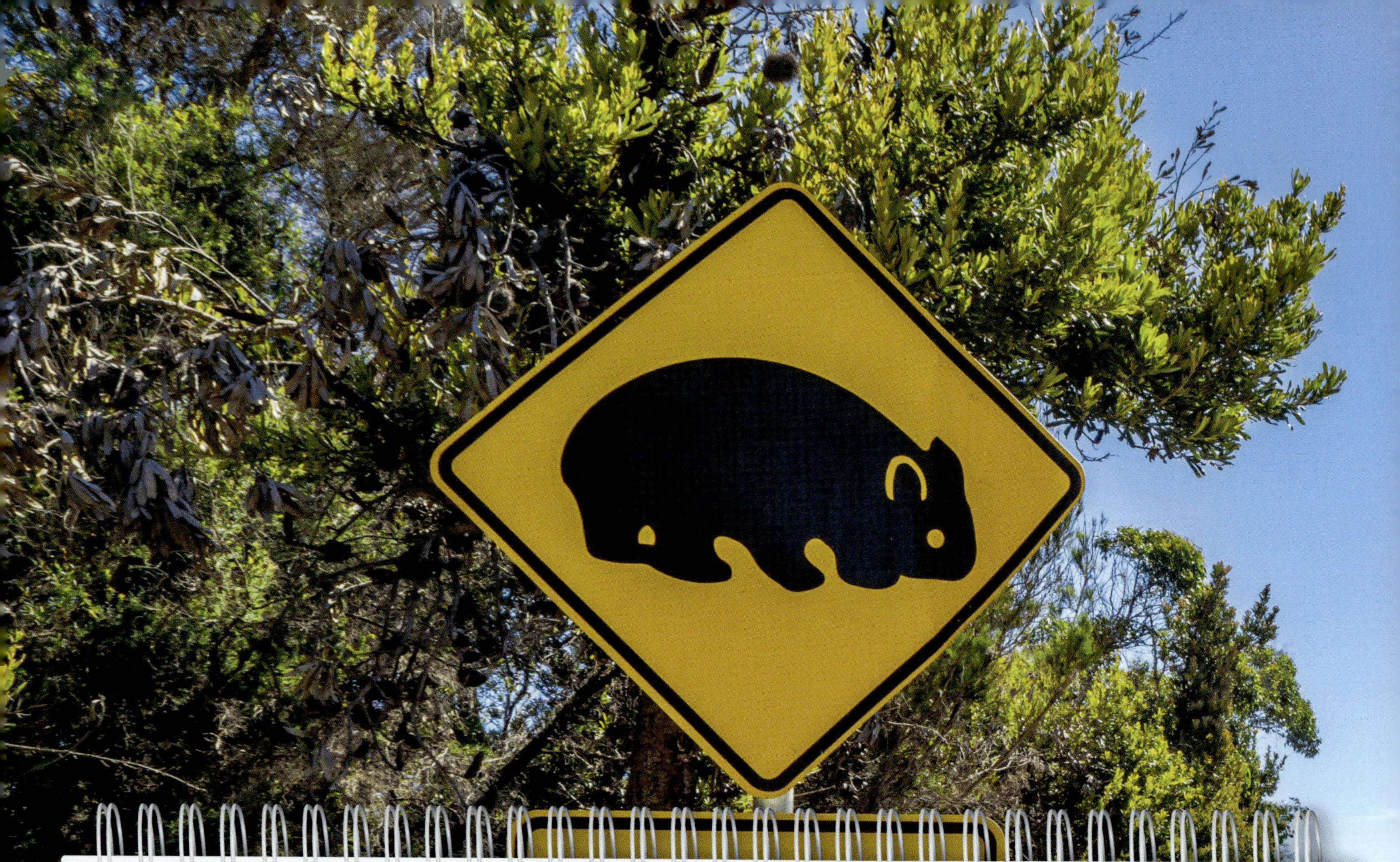

First Published 2024 by
Redback Publishing
Suite 6, 13a Narabang Way,
Belrose NSW 2085
Australia

www.redbackpublishing.com
info@redbackpublishing.com

ISBN 978-1-761400-71-1

Author: John Lesley
Editor: Caroline Thomas
Design: Redback Publishing

A catalogue record for this book is available from the National Library of Australia

Original illustrations © Redback Publishing 2024
Originated by Redback Publishing

Acknowledgements
Abbreviations: l—left, r—right,
b—bottom, t—top, c—centre, m—middle
We would like to thank the following for permission to reproduce photographs: (Images © shutterstock)
pg21mr Torpy/Shutterstock.com, pg24ml ARC CoE CABAH, CC BY-SA 4.0 <https://creativecommons.org/licenses/by-sa/4.0>, via Wikimedia Commons, og24br Ryan Somma, CC BY-SA 2.0 <https://creativecommons.org/licenses/by-sa/2.0>, via Wikimedia Commons, pg25tr Danny Ye/Shutterstock.com, pg27tr ellinnur bakarudin/Shutterstock.com

CONTENTS

WHAT IS A WOMBAT?

The wombat is an Australian marsupial. It looks like a little bear, but it is not related to bears from other parts of the world. The wombat's closest relative is actually the koala.

Wombats are short and stocky, with a large head, strong claws and thick fur. They usually move around slowly with a wobbling, lumbering style of walking, but they can also run very fast if they have to.

Wombats have a reputation for not being very smart, but this is not the case. They are perfectly adapted to their habitats and have thrived in Australia for millions of years.

BURROWS

Wombats dig long burrows, sometimes under houses, where they snore as they sleep under the floorboards.

MARSUPIALS

Australia is the continent of marsupials, and wombats are just one of over 300 types of marsupials still surviving there.

In the past, there were many more species of marsupials living in every habitat across Australia. As with all wildlife, habitat loss and human activities have restricted the range of places where wombats can exist in the wild.

Marsupials are a type of mammal that has these characteristics:
The mother produces milk to feed the young
They have fur or hair
The females give birth to tiny, underdeveloped babies (baby wombats are called joeys)
The babies crawl to the mother's pouch, or special fold of skin, and do the rest of their growing there (baby wombats stay in the pouch for eight months)

WOMBAT BASIC FACTS

WHERE

Wombats are only found in Australia, where they are the country's biggest, burrowing marsupial.

NAME

The name 'wombat' probably comes from an Indigenous Australian Dharug word. In the past, colonists thought wombats looked like European badgers, which is the origin of the numerous place-names across Australia that start with the name 'Badger', such as Badger Creek and Badger Hill.

SOUNDS

Adult wombats make a grumbling noise, or they may growl and hiss at each other. A mother wombat and her baby make a soft, grunting noise which helps them to know where the other is and to stay together.

CONSERVATION STATUS

The common wombat is not under threat of extinction at present, although its numbers have declined as more of their habitat is taken by people for buildings and farming.

The southern and the northern hairy-nosed wombats are not as safe from extinction, and their numbers are declining.

WOMBAT BODY

SIZE AND SHAPE

Wombats can grow to be large and heavy, with some being over one metre long and weighing over thirty kilograms. They have thick fur that varies in colour from light grey to brown or black.

A wombat's head is very sturdy, which helps when they are digging burrows. The large, rounded rump is used as a barrier to protect the burrow from intruders.

TEETH

Wombat teeth keep growing, so they need to eat a lot of tough plant food to keep the teeth from getting too long. There are two cutting teeth at the front of the jaw, and flatter teeth at the back for grinding up plants.

CLAWS

The wombat's claws are long and strong. They use them for digging burrows, and to protect themselves from predators.

POUCH

The female wombat's pouch faces backwards. This stops dirt from the front claws being pushed in on top of the joey when its mother is making the burrow.

DEFENCES

The wombat may appear to be slow and defenceless, but it can be a dangerous animal. The long front teeth that usually bite off pieces of plants can also be used to bite into a predator. The claws are strong enough to cause serious injury and to dig deep burrows.

Wombats can run when they need to, either to escape a predator or to run towards one and drive it away.

The rear claws are adapted for grooming the thick fur and removing parasites. The claws on the two middle toes of the hindfoot are joined together and can reach nearly every part of the body to scratch and groom.

THREE TYPES OF WOMBAT

There are three different types of wombat in Australia:

LITTLE BEAR

The species name, *ursinus*, means that it looks like a little bear.

1. COMMON WOMBAT

Vombatus ursinus

- As its name suggests, this is the most common wombat in Australia.
- Also called the bare-nosed wombat, since no hair grows on the end of its large nose.
- Lives in eastern Australia, including Tasmania.

EXTINCTION

This species is now in danger of imminent extinction.

2. NORTHERN HAIRY-NOSED WOMBAT

Lasiorhinus krefftii

- This is the largest wombat species alive today, and the largest burrowing marsupial anywhere.
- Lives only in a few parts of Queensland.

3. SOUTHERN HAIRY-NOSED WOMBAT

Lasiorhinus latifrons

- The ears are larger and more pointed than those of the common wombat.
- Under threat of extinction.
- Lives in parts of South Australia, with very few left in Western Australia and New South Wales.

WOMBAT HABITAT

Wombats live only in Australia. They used to be very widespread, living in most environments except for deserts and dense, tropical rainforests. Wombats can become overheated, so they avoid the hottest part of the day and they do not live in very hot, dry areas.

They are now only found in the eastern and southern parts of Australia, where they live in semi-arid areas, grasslands, dry forests, alpine regions and in farmers' paddocks.

Wombats have territories which may extend for many hectares. If there is plenty of plant food available, the territory of each wombat will be smaller, and it is then possible to see many wombat burrows not far from each other.

Wombats prefer to go out to feed at nighttime or on overcast days. They like to build their burrow in a shaded area, such as in a gully beside a creek and overhung with trees.

WOMBAT LIFE CYCLE

MATING

Wombats are mostly solitary animals. The male and female come together to mate, but at other times they will drive each other away from their own territory.

LIFESPAN

In the wild, wombats probably live for up to ten to fifteen years. In captivity, they live well over twenty years.

JOEY

Usually, only one joey is born, but wombats can have twins. As with all marsupials, the young joey looks embryonic but has well-developed front limbs. Using these, it crawls into the female's pouch and attaches itself to a teat. Living on milk until it grows enough teeth to eat plants, the baby stays in the pouch for about eight months.

After growing too big for the pouch, the joey follows its mother around for another few months, before it goes off to claim its own territory.

WHAT THEY EAT

Wombats are herbivores, which means that they eat plants, grasses, bushes and plant roots. Because their teeth keep growing throughout their life, wombats seek out tough plant foods so that their teeth are constantly worn down and do not grow too long.

REC
4K UHD
3...2...1... 1...2...3
00:35:02
Wombats come out of their burrows at night to forage for food.
During cool, overcast days, wombats will also come out to feed during the daytime. In forested areas, where the trees create a canopy that blocks the sunlight, wombats may come out every day to feed.
4K UHD

THREATS TO WOMBATS

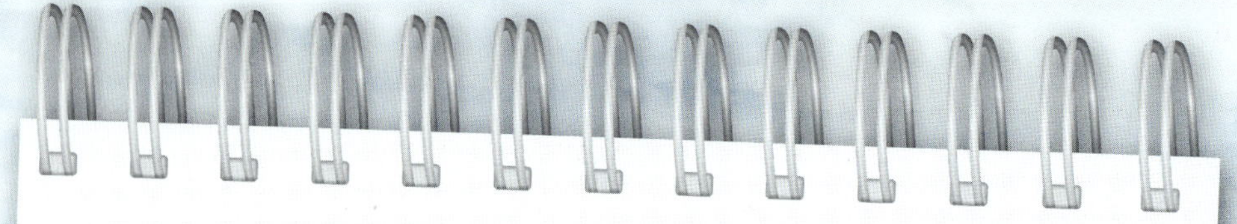

HABITAT LOSS

Wombats were once one of the most common marsupials in Australia. As people build towns and take more areas for farming, this reduces the habitat available for wombats.

In some areas, wombats have adapted to the conversion of natural grasslands to farms by digging their burrows in paddocks or under buildings.

MANGE

Mange is a skin problem caused by an infestation of tiny insects called mites. Many furred animals get mange, including pet dogs and cats. Wombats with mange lose their fur and become very sick.

PREDATORS

Dingoes, feral dogs and cats prey on wombats, and large eagles will attempt to take a baby wombat. These predators seek out the young and the sick wombats, which are easiest to catch.

HUMANS

In the past, farmers in Australia used to be allowed to kill wombats, which were considered a pest that ruined farmland with burrows. Wombats are now protected and cannot be harmed or taken from the wild, except in a few exceptional circumstances.

Wombats are notorious for being able to burrow under any fencing that farmers put around their land.

WOMBATS AND PEOPLE

TAME OR WILD?

If raised from a joey, a wombat can become tame, but its wild cousins should not be approached. Even though a fictional story might portray them as cuddly, a wild wombat will defend its territory and react to any approach by a human as a threat. They may chase and attack humans who venture too close to them.

ROADS

Wombats can often be found dead beside a road after being hit by a car or truck. As with all Australian wildlife, they have no defences against fast vehicles.

FAMOUS WOMBATS

Wombats have become well-known and much-loved as characters in television shows and children's books. Portrayed as charming and friendly, these wombats have become ambassadors for their species, even though they often don't portray the lifestyle or character of wild wombats.

SHOOTING

Some governments in Australia will allow farmers to destroy wombats if they are damaging property by burrowing in the soil. Recreational hunting of wombats is strictly forbidden.

GIANT WOMBATS

PHASCOLONUS

Phascolonus was a giant but distant relative of wombats. It lived millions of years ago, including through the Ice Age. It seems to have become extinct only about 40,000 years ago, so it would have been encountered by Australia's Indigenous people.

Phascolonus may have weighed as much as a medium-sized crocodile, but its fossilised teeth suggest it was a herbivore, like modern wombats. *Phascolonus* is one example of the many types of megafauna that used to live all across Australia.

Illustration of *Phascolonus gigas*

Phascolonus

DIPROTODON

Diprotodon optatum was a prehistoric giant and an ancient relative of both wombats and koalas. It grew to four metres long and had huge front teeth, very much like those of the modern wombat, only bigger. Diprotodon was also part of the megafauna and lived in Australia at the same time as *Phascolonus*.

Although usually referred to as a giant wombat, *Diprotodon* was not closely related, although it possibly did look like an enormous relative.

MEGAFAUNA

The Australian megafauna were gigantic animals that lived up until about 40,000 years ago. Although they had existed for millions of years, the Australian megafauna all became extinct within only a few thousand years. This extinction was possibly due to a combination of climate change and being hunted by humans.

There are some megafauna in Africa that managed to avoid extinction. These include elephants and the rhinoceros.

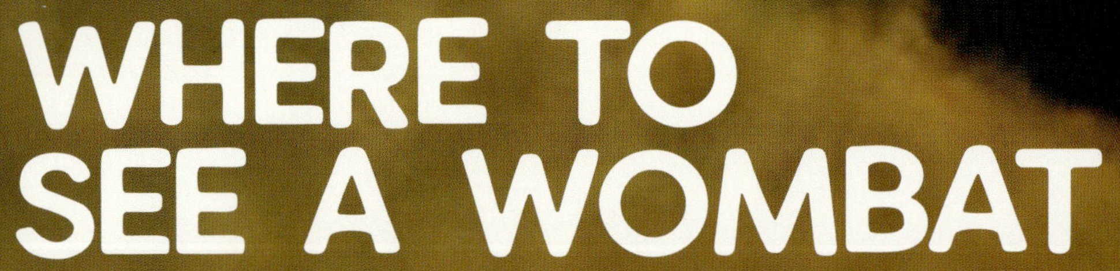

WHERE TO SEE A WOMBAT

IN THE WILD

The bare-nosed wombat is not rare. A quiet, careful bushwalker can often see them in the wild. Evenings are the best time.

On farmland where there are many burrows, wombats might come out in the evenings to feed on nearby grasses. Do not approach a wild wombat, as they can be very aggressive and fast.

ZOOS

Wombats have sharp claws and will bite, but patting a tame wombat is sometimes offered as a special zoo experience for human visitors.

Wombats in zoos are limited in the size of the burrow they can dig. In the wild, burrows can be many metres long, but this is not possible in a zoo environment.

SORTING ANIMALS INTO GROUPS

Biologists divide all living things around the world into groups. They call this process classification.

The two basic groups of animals are called:

INVERTEBRATES
Invertebrates do not have a backbone

VERTEBRATES
Vertebrates have a backbone

BIRDS (AVES)

Vertebrates are further divided into five groups called classes.

MAMMALS (MAMMALIA)

FISH

AMPHIBIANS (AMPHIBIA)

REPTILES (REPTILIA)

Wombats are mammals and belong in the class called Mammalia.
Mammals are further divided into three groups:
MARSUPIALS
MONOTREMES
PLACENTALS
Wombats are in the group called marsupials.
Humans have a place in this animal classification too. We are mammals and placentals.

POO CUBES?

It's true! Wombats really do produce poo that is shaped like little cubes.

Wombats have a very slow digestion rate. This results in the poo being quite dry. Wombats have probably evolved to turn this dry poo into cubes as a way of leaving messages around their territory for other wombats to read through smell. The cubic shape would allow the message to be neatly stacked and not roll away.

The cubes are made by muscles pressing on the poo at the end of the wombat's intestines.

GLOSSARY

abundant having a lot available

embryonic referring to an underdeveloped baby not yet born

forage search for food

groom (verb) look after the hair on a body

hind foot foot on a back leg

imminent about to happen soon

intestines internal tube that digests food

lumbering walking slowly and with difficulty

marsupial mammal that feeds its underdeveloped babies on milk and keeps them in a pouch on the female's body

notorious famous for something bad

rump rear part of a mammal

species separate types of animals

stocky short, rounded shape

sturdy strong and not easy to damage

venture (verb) try to do something difficult

INDEX